CHART HITS NOW!

WE ARE YOUNG

...PLUS 11 MORE TOP HITS

WISE PUBLICATIONS
part of The Music Sales Group
London / New York / Paris / Sydney / Copenhagen / Berlin / Madrid / Hong Kong / Tokyo

Published by
Wise Publications
14-15 Berners Street, London W1T 3LJ, UK.

Exclusive Distributors:

Music Sales Limited
Distribution Centre, Newmarket Road,
Bury St Edmunds, Suffolk IP33 3YB, UK.

Music Sales Pty Limited
20 Resolution Drive, Caringbah,
NSW 2229, Australia.

Order No. AM1005576
ISBN: 978-1-78038-744-4
This book © Copyright 2012 Wise Publications,
a division of Music Sales Limited.

Edited by Jenni Norey.
Cover design by Tim Field.

Printed in the EU.

Boyfriend

Words & Music by Justin Bieber, Mike Posner,
Matthew Musto & Mason Levy

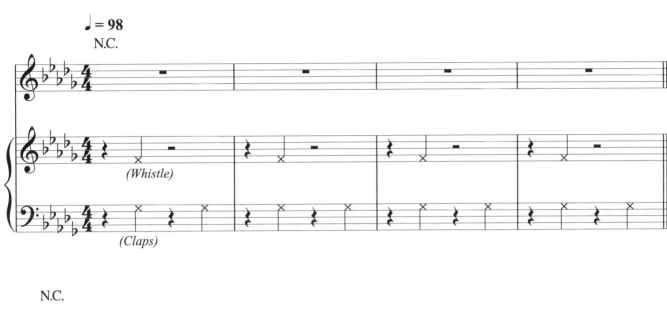

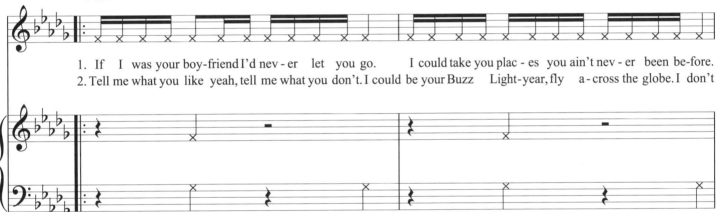

1. If I was your boy-friend I'd nev - er let you go. I could take you plac - es you ain't nev - er been be-fore.
2. Tell me what you like yeah, tell me what you don't. I could be your Buzz Light-year, fly a-cross the globe. I don't

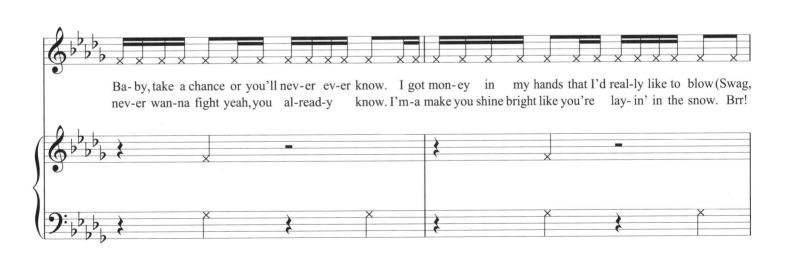

Ba - by, take a chance or you'll nev-er ev-er know. I got mon-ey in my hands that I'd real-ly like to blow (Swag,
nev-er wan-na fight yeah, you al-read-y know. I'm-a make you shine bright like you're lay-in' in the snow. Brr!

4

Keep you on my arm____ girl,____ you'd nev - er be a - lone.____

I could be a gen - tle - man,____ an - y - thing you want.____

To Coda ⊕

If I was your boy - friend,____ I'd nev - er let you go.____

1.

I'd nev - er let you go. ____

2.

I'd nev - er let you go.____

6

Chasing The Sun

Words & Music by Elliot Gleave & Alex Smith

Lyrics:
1. I'm bet - ter, so much bet - ter now. I see the light, touch the
sun. 2. I'm nev - er, I'm nev - er down, ly - ing here star - ing

9

sun.
day - light's fad - ing we're gon-na play in the dark till it's gold - en a - gain.

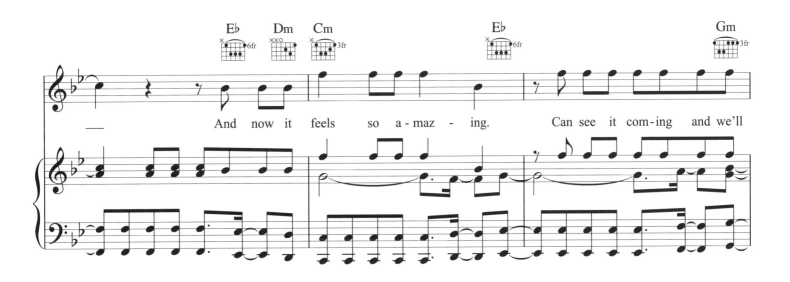

And now it feels so a - maz - ing. Can see it com-ing and we'll

D.S. al Coda

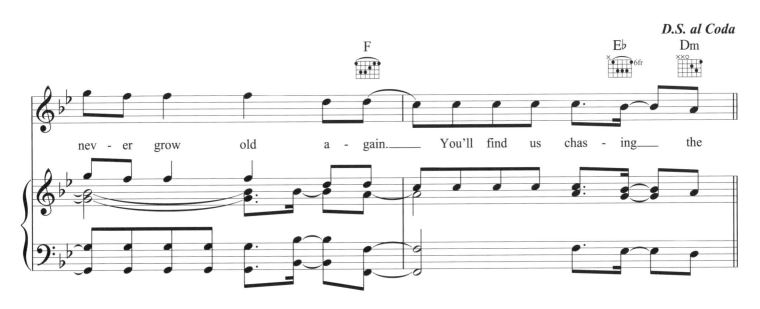

nev - er grow old a - gain. You'll find us chas - ing the

12

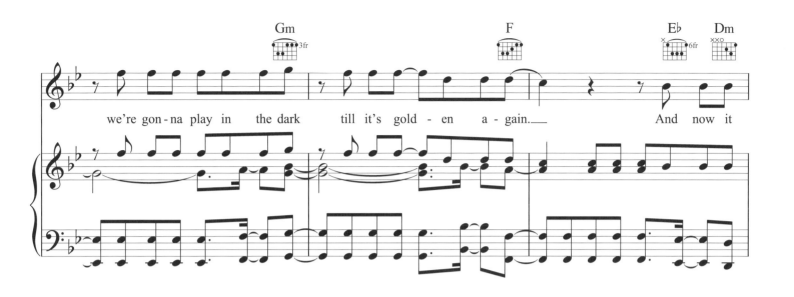

we're gon-na play in the dark till it's gold-en a-gain.___ And now it

feels so a-maz - ing. Can see it com-ing and we'll nev-er grow old a-gain.___

___ You'll find us chas-ing___ the sun.
Oh._____

14

You'll find us chas - ing_ the sun. Oh, oh, oh, oh, oh,_ oh._ Oh, oh, oh, oh,_ oh._

1.

_ Oh, oh, oh, oh, oh,_ oh._ You'll find us chas - ing_ the

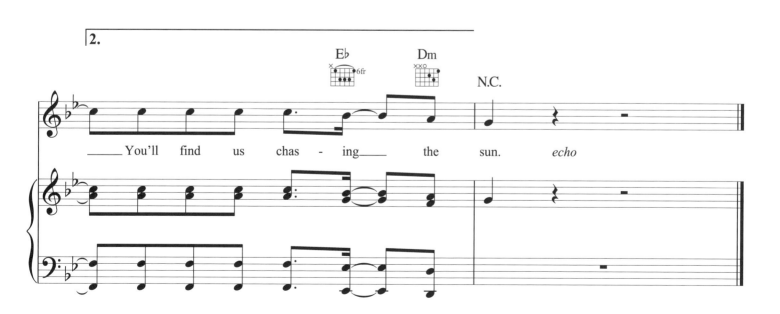

2.

You'll find us chas - ing the sun. _echo_

Laserlight

Words & Music by George Astasio, Jason Pebworth, Jonathan Shave, David Guetta,
Frédéric Riesterer, Giorgio Tuinfort & Jessica Cornish

18

safe. You know I would-n't have it an - y oth - er way.

(D - D - D - D - Da - vid G.)

(Je-Je - Je - Je - Jes - sie J.)

2. You and me,

24

More Than This

Words & Music by Jamie Scott

I'm blind - ed__ 'cause you are ev - 'ry - thing__ I__ see.__
I'm pray - ing__ that your heart will__ just turn__ a - round.__

And as I walk__ up to__ your door__ my head turns__ to face__ the floor.__

__ 'Cause I can't look__ you in__ the eyes__ and say... When he

o - pens his arms__ and holds__ you close to - night__ it just won't feel__ right.__
lays you down__ I might__ just die__ in - side,__ it just don't feel__ right.__

26

And then I see___ you on___ the street___ in his arms.___ I___ get weak,__

___ my bod - y fails,___ I'm on___ my knees___ pray - ing. When he

o - pens his arms___ and holds___ you close___ to - night___ it just won't feel___ right.
lays you down___ I might___ just die___ in - side, it just don't feel___ right.

'Cause I can love___ you more___ than this.___ Yeah.___ When he Yeah.___

28

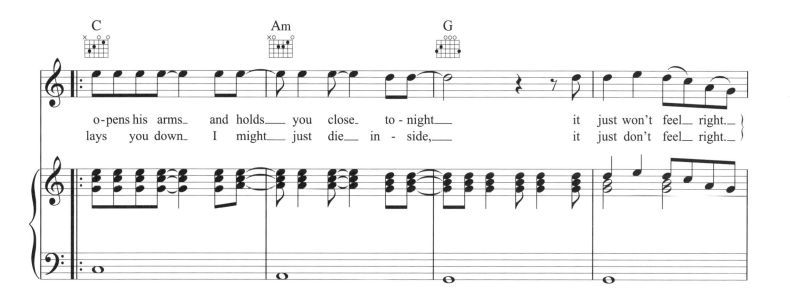

o-pens his arms__ and holds___ you close_ to-night___ it just won't feel_ right.
lays you down__ I might___ just die__ in - side,___ it just don't feel_ right.

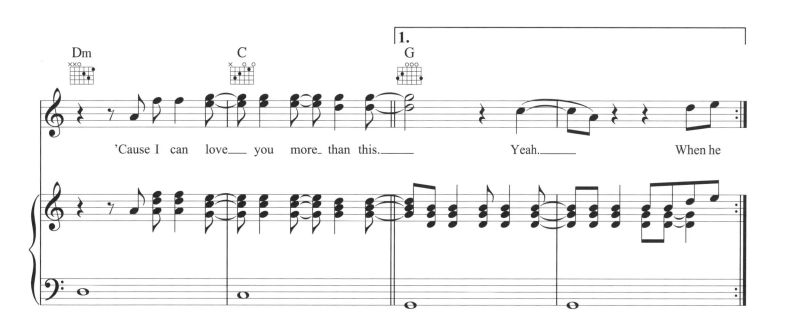

'Cause I can love___ you more_ than this.___ Yeah.___ When he

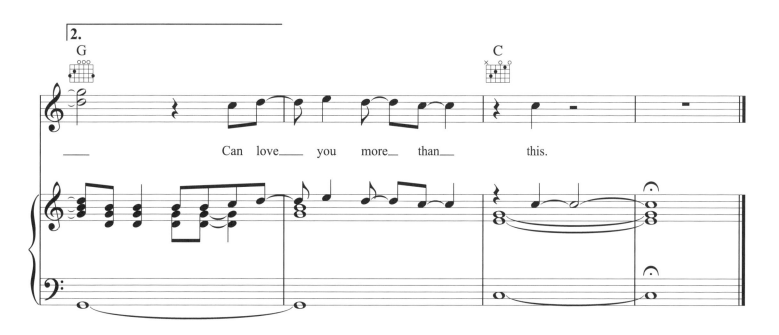

___ Can love___ you more_ than___ this.

R.I.P.

Words & Music by Mikkel Eriksen, Tor Erik Hermansen, Saul Milton, William Kennard,
Aubrey Graham, Patrick Okogwu, Renee Wisdom & Nneka Egbuna

33

Thought it o - ver and de - cid - ed to - night is your
Men - tal pic - tures, no cam - 'ras please.

night.
Vocal ad lib.

To Coda ⊕

R. I. P. to the girl you used to see.___ Her days are

Shake It Out

Words & Music by
Paul Epworth, Florence Welch & Tom Hull

47

Someone Like You

Words & Music by Adele Adkins & Daniel Wilson

found a girl___ and you're mar-ried now._____
yes-ter-day___ was the time of our lives._____ We were

I heard___ that your dreams came true. Guess she
born and raised___ in a sum-mer haze. Bound

gave you things___ I did-n't give to you._____
by the sur-prise of our glo-ry days. I

1° only

Old friend, why are you so___ shy?_ Ain't like

you to hold back, or hide from the light. I
hate to turn up out of the blue un-in-vit-ed but I could-n't stay a-way. I could-n't fight it. I had
hoped you'd see my face and that you'd be re-mind-ed that for me it is-n't o - ver.

1° only

2° only

Nev-er mind I'll find_ some-one like_ you._____ I wish

noth-ing but_ the best_ for____ you two. Don't for -

-get me, I beg._ I'll_ re - mem-ber_____ you said____ some-times it

1, 3.

lasts and loves but some-times it hurts in - stead._____ Some-times it

Too Close

Words & Music by Jim Duguid & Alex Clare

1. You know I'm not one to break prom-is-es.

I don't wan-na hurt you but I need to breathe.

2. At the end of it all, you're still my best friend.
3. You've giv-en me more than I can re-turn.

But there's some-thing in-side that I need to re-lease.
Yet there's oh, so much that you de-serve.

Video Games

Words & Music by Elizabeth Grant & Justin Parker

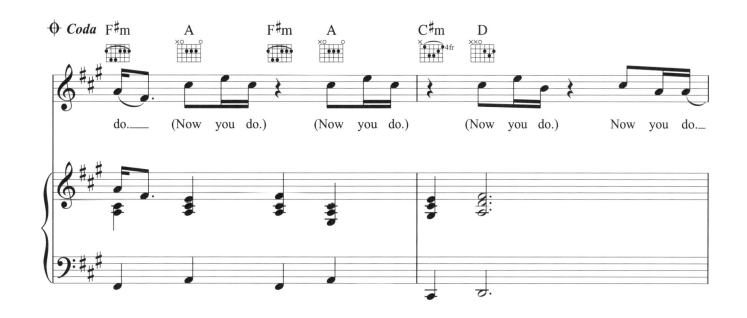

do.____ (Now you do.) (Now you do.) (Now you do.) Now you do.__

__ (Now, now you do.) (Now you do.) (Now you do.)__

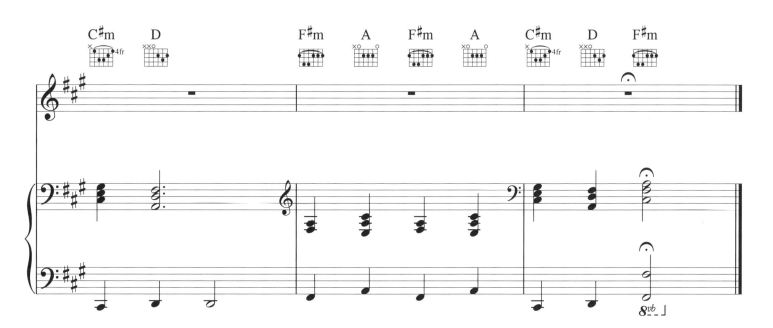

We Are Young

Words & Music by Jeff Bhasker, Nate Ruess,
Andrew Dost & Jack Antonoff

1.Give me a se-cond I, I need to get__ my sto-ry straight. My friends are in the bath-room get-ting

high-er than the Em-pire State. My lo-ver she is wait-ing for me just a-cross the bar.__ My seat's been

The world is on my side,___ I have no rea-son to run. So will some-one come and

car - ry me home to - night.___ The an-gels nev- er ar - rived___ but I can hear the choir.

So will some-one come and car - ry me home.___ To - night___ we___ are___ young.___

So let's set the world on

Write It On Your Skin

Words & Music by Newton Faulkner

All the things I'd ra - ther be.____

I can't, I can't, I can't stay a - round__ here.

I can on - ly leave.____

Take ev - 'ry - thing you__

can't get off. And life feels like a mu-sic box. I'm
(Let's start a - gain.)____ (Start a - gain.)__

spin-ning 'round slow-ly and I can't get off. And can't get off.
____ (Let's start a - gain.)____

Coda

I____ can't, I____ can't, I____ can't stay a - round____ here.

Young

Words & Music by
Lorne Tennant, Richard Rawson & Peter Ibsen

(Ooh,_____ ah.)_   (Ooh,_____ ah.)_

1. For - give me for what I have done,   'cause I'm
2. I'll make mis - takes that I learn   from,   'cause I'm

young,   yeah, I'm__ young.   For - give me for what I have done,
young,   yeah, I'm__ young.   I'm sor - ry you're not e - ven done,

'cause I'm young, yeah, I'm young.
'cause I'm young, yeah, I'm young. I Don't

don't mean to fright-en you off, it's just fun. It's just
wor - ry 'bout what I'll be - come, it's just fun. It's just

fun. I don't mean to fright-en you off, it's just
fun. I scream at the top of my lungs, it's just

fun, it's just fun.
fun, it's just fun.

(Ooh, ah.)

N.C.

76

'cause we're young,___ we're young,___ we're young.___

N.C.

Instrumental ad lib.

(Drums)

N.C.

1.

123456789